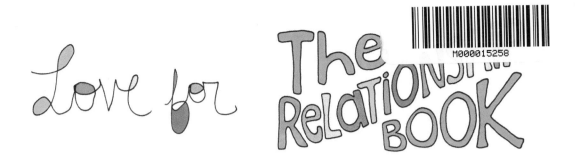

Love for The Relationship Book

"Rachel's book is a giant love generator whirling through your heart and awakening your fresh vision. Steep, bask in, and savor these profound pages of art and words; be uplifted by the shapes and sounds which will arise mightily to inspire your very own life."

SARK, artist, author, and inspirationalist at PlanetSARK.com

"A jolt of life force straight to my entire being! Reading *The Relationship Book* was an extraordinary experience. With each page turned, I felt myself waking up to a version of myself that wanted to be not only remembered, but resurrected.

Rachel's writing, combined with her brilliant illustrations, moved me so deeply that I felt an immediate and inspired call to action: To tend to my relationship to myself and others with a sense of reverent playfulness and creative joy. This book is so special and the best ever—I could not put it down. HOLY SMOKES."

Kelly Rae Roberts, artist and possibilitarian at kellyraeroberts.com

"*The Relationship Book* encourages us all to cultivate a life in which we show up proudly and with pizzazz, in both our radiance and our brokenness, inspiring others to also walk their truest path. What a magical gift to the world Rachel brings with this uplifting missive of juicy, lavish self-nourishment!"

Tracy Verdugo, author, prolific painter, beauty seeker, worldwide teacher, and inspiration instigator at tracyverdugo.com

The Relationship Book

A Soulful, Transformational, and Artistic
Invent🌸ry of Your Connective Life

Words
&
pictures
by
Rachel Awes, MA, LP.

Delivered straight to your heart

ISBN 13: 978-1-63489-568-2

Library of Congress Catalog Number has been applied for.
Printed in the United States of America
First Printing: 2022

26 25 24 23 22   5 4 3 2 1

Illustrations by Rachel Awes
Book Design by Rachel Awes and Patrick Maloney

Wise Ink Creative Publishing
807 Broadway St. NE
Suite 46
Minneapolis, MN 55413

www.rachelawes.com

rachelawes@gmail.com

"All I really really want
our love to do
is to
bring out the best
in me
and
in you
too."

—Joni Mitchell

Table of Contents

Introduction

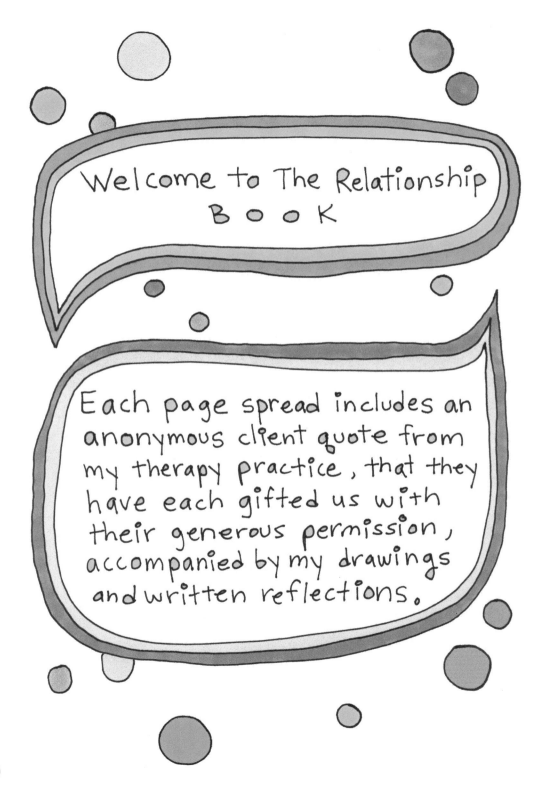

Welcome to The Relationship
B O O K

Each page spread includes an
anonymous client quote from
my therapy practice, that they
have each gifted us with
their generous permission,
accompanied by my drawings
and written reflections.

You will notice that most of the time, the faces don't include eyes, noses, and mouths. I call them "listening faces", drawn for you to see your own life in them. I did, however, include the eyes, noses, + mouths on the animals, because they told me to (in my heart.)

The soft velvety invitation held in all of these pages is for you to become the person you want to be with, and that all of your relationships would flow out of that place.

As you feel moved, go ahead and find a cozy spot to read. Maybe put on some tea, and a robe and slippers (or bare feet.) Pay attention to what feels good to you; perhaps a lit candle, an open window, sitting outside, music, silence, reading out loud with a friend, journaling alongside, doodling in the book, hearing your own breath as you read.

I am dearly glad you are here, alive, in this world, with yourself, with these pages, with me, and with all living and breathing creatures. Our connections with one another are astounding and powerful, and I offer my gratitude today and always for you and me.
♥ Love, Rachel

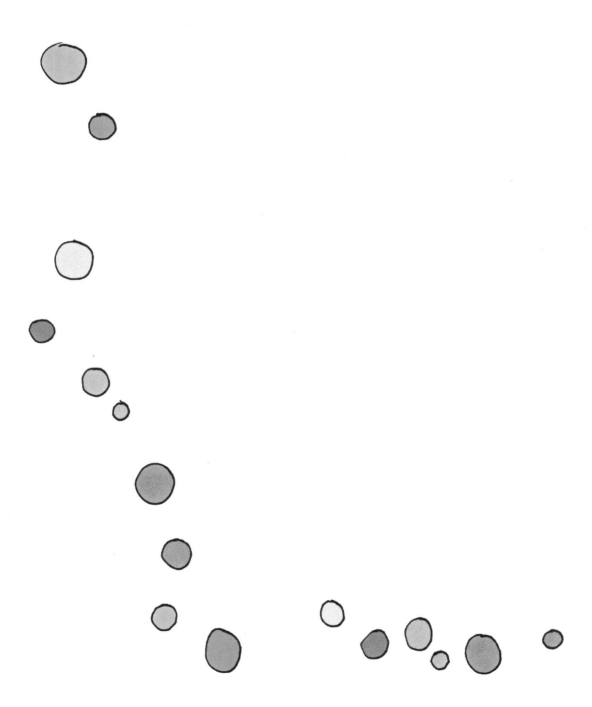

one

Relationship with myself

"One of my goals is to become the person I want to be with."

I Do

I am speaking words of gratitude, knowing this will create in me more joy and kindness. I am breathing in elegance and innocence, knitting together my becoming and my beginning. I am deliberate in building my strength, rooting me to this earth and to this great gift of life. I am expanding my vision of what is possible, dissolving old messages of smallness. I am leaning within and listening, knowing and trusting my wild and beautiful resources. I am loyal to my inner child, who is vulnerable and sometimes afraid. I am tending to her, guiding and loving her, and learning from her.

I am honoring all parts of me. I am bringing my whole self flowers, and often. I am affirming her and saying to her that she is who I want to be with. I am telling her yes and I love you and I do.

Gratitude

There lives a particular place inside where I sometimes stay and savor the moment. Like the time I ate a pear and set the remaining core on my lawn. Like how a wild bunny materialized in less than a minute to finish it. Like how just thinking about this shared meal with such a soft and nibbling creature became elation. Like how my heart turned into a soft and silky thing. Like how my neck and shoulder muscles melted into oneness with the magic of this world, as they inevitably do, when I am mindful enough to pause long enough and say thank you.

" When asked how I am, I reply with saying I am grateful. "

"I want
to live into
my
elegance
+
innocence."

Elegance and Innocence

I wish to stitch and knit
and braid and parade
forward, all that
I am, breathing
in and honoring
my elegance and
innocence, and fall
in mad love with
how beautiful my
wholeness looks on me.

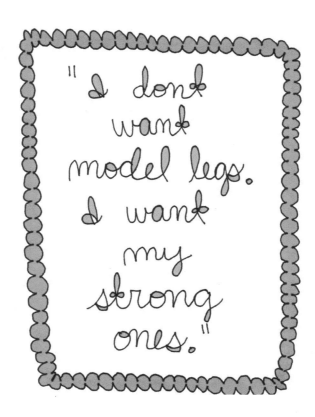

"I don't want model legs. I want my strong ones."

I Want What I Have

I want what I have. At least I want to want to, and I trust in my "want to want to" kind of power.

I consciously choose my strong legs, rooting me to this earth and to this great gift of life. I also wish all living creatures this same want to want to power. For all body types. To profess yes to our true frame.

The trunk of a tree knows this with its form holding invaluable offerings of leaves and fruits and flowers. Where would the birds and elephants and whole universe be without them?

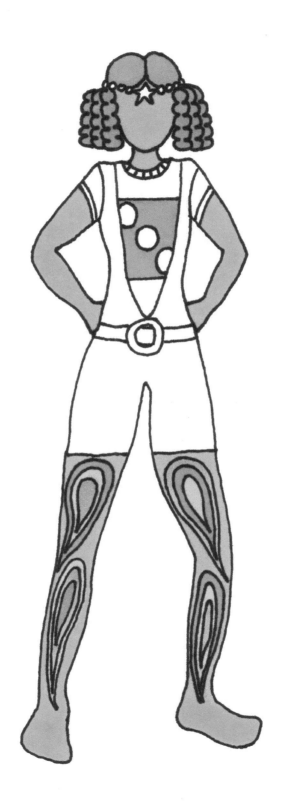

Break Free

I wish to break free from the Land of Narrow. Break out of believing I have only two options. Expand my menu from either scrambling or frying my eggs, to having a grocery aisle of options, the whole store, entire fields to graze from.

I move forward with panoramic eyes. Seeing big space. Bound for the boundless. Knowing the infinite resides deep inside, like big Montana sky. The place where wings stretch wide.

The unconfined is calling.

"Anytime I'm stuck between two things, I recall there's three other options in the middle."

Return to My Own Words

Time after time I have searched for someone else's fitting and lovely poem to write inside a greeting card. Multitudes are available, and yet without fail, I lay down the outer search and return to my own words. My own vulnerability. Owning my messy and splendid expression and allowing connection to flow from this place.

I hold my inner encounter dear. With each glimpse, I see greens growing, sprigs sprouting, my heart softening. Why would I not trust such a place? Why would I not wish to visit often?

I open myself to the flow of my inner knowing. To this garden. To this place of immeasurable offerings.

" I try to remember to first check within before looking for answers outside of me."

" my inner child is afraid of my next steps ahead & I'm pointing out to her

Right Radar

I am loyal to my inner child, who is vulnerable and sometimes afraid. I am tending to her, guiding and loving her, and learning from her.

She is pure of heart. She tells the truth. Her radar is right. She says "I want this" and "I don't like that." She knows the socks that gladden. She selects foods she fancies. She pinpoints desired pals on the playground. She runs down the block because her body feels like running.

28

she's gotten
this far
leaning into
her strength
+
I'll be with her
as she
keeps stepping."

She can also be afraid of what shows up on her path.
Lions and tigers and bears.

I remind her that she is a lion and tiger and bear. I tell
her she stands just as tall by knowing what she loves. It is
no small thing to pluck desired socks out of a drawer. To
select the life you want. And I will keep letting her, rooting
her on, and be snug as a bug by her side.

This Heart

There is a great kindness residing in the heart of me, speaking softly when I feel vulnerable and in need of protection.

In moments when I might run away or speak sharply or freeze, this heart compassionately knows I am trying to take care of myself. She knows I am doing the best I can. The music from this organ plays me unconditional lyrics of "good job" and "I understand."

Any need to fix or solve or improve melts away. All that remains is loving tenderness, and that is enough.

"In response to my
big emotions
lately,
I'm placing
my hand
on my
brain stem
& saying
'good job
trying
to protect me.'"

"I've named the nervous part of myself 'The Purple Guy' + am working on hearing him + being good to him."

A Cast of Characters

I open my cape and a cast of characters flocks forward. Each Emmy awarded and deep heart applauded. There is "The Purple Guy" who is always nervous, "Gladys" who always feels she must put on a glad face, and "Candy" who invariably asks for more candy. There are many others with hands waving excitedly in the air, waiting for their day to be chosen, named, and brought into the fold.

These are the parts of me who I laugh with and lounge with, cry with and hold, rest with and wrestle with, reconcile with and release, and do it all over again. Seeing them outside of me gives me a new way to introduce myself to myself. I then seem to show up with better manners, treating myself with more care.

At the close of the day, I tuck them in and whisper sweet dreams and tell them I'll see them again in the morning.

"I'm feeling more depressed & am realizing I need to create more

Wild and Beautiful

When standard self-care practices aren't sustaining my well-being, I turn to experiences that are wild and beautiful.

I walk in the rain. Picnic behind a waterfall. Build a treehouse. Flambé some food. Knit sweaters for trees. Watch the sunrise from a hot air

experiences that are wild & beautiful."

balloon. Show up at a friend's door and sing. Read poetry at midnight. Write to an elephant. Say a purring prayer with a tiger at the zoo.

Somehow these all get inside of me and work their magic. Can you see the colorful hot air balloons traveling around now in my breath? How about the elephant inside my palm who is writing me back?

Open Fields

Sometimes I thirst for open fields and no home. Setting out for a road trip with wind and no comb.

Where meadows are for dancing and watching the stars. Where tambourines are for playing wherever we are.

Where clothing only speaks of the fanciful free, and people are released to all be who they be.

"i've got a bit of the gypsy in me."

"My new goal for everything: check first if it's interesting, goofy, & beautiful."

Whole Selves

There is much consideration given these days to taking care of the body, mind, and spirit.

I also want to imagine additional ways to acknowledge and care for my whole presence, like how I house a trio of the interesting, goofy, and beautiful. Maybe care for these by assembling Play-Doh petunias, waltz in my polka-dot pajamas, grow a garden of gnomes.

I hear the interesting, goofy, and beautiful as having harmonic voices, and as I care for all three, my heart sings itself sillyingly whole.

The Prettiest Day

Today's sunrise is winsome, birds are flying miracles, and pouring rains never sounded so pretty. The phone ringing is my chance to say a kind thing. Tears are here to heal me. A guitar, ukulele, and harp lie at my feet, and I could play any of their strings. I see growing things all around me like dandelions and trees, and see falling things too, like the night and the dew. Each encounter's a dance, and every breath the music.

This day is so pretty that all I name really does come true.

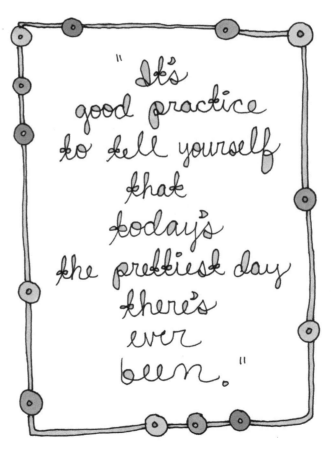

"It's good practice to tell yourself that today's the prettiest day there's ever been."

These

Dahlias, azaleas, and daisies, these are the flowers for me.

Lilacs, lilies, and bluebells are the bestest that best can be.

Marigolds, mums, and zinnias are the dreamiest bloomiest too, and roses, tulips, and orchids are the love in "I love you."

"I signed up to have weekly flowers delivered to me this summer."

> " my new mantra
> is :
> mistake,
> mistake,
> mistake,
> &
> still go
> forward
> & trust
> my voice. "

A Planet

I'm like a planet spinning wildly and purposefully in starry space, with sparking zings and zangs of mistakes and marvels shooting out of me. Colorful wisdom born out of suffering and wrestling is twirling and whirling around my surface. New pinks and blues are emerging that have never been here before.

This is my active becoming. The real picture. A mad hatter's cooking show with rapid boiling and simmering and everything in between.

This is not a reason to doubt my voice. This provides every reason to trust it.

Relationship with myself

Questions to row your boat with, to know and not (yet) know with. Questions to write your songs with, and closely walk your life with. Questions to tea party and book club with, and share or not (yet) share with. Questions to journal and meditate with, and lie down at angels' feet with. Questions only you know how to bring you best along with:

What occurs to me when I consider wanting to become the person I want to be with? How would I describe such a person? Would I treat myself any differently? What might I begin and what might I end, or maybe adjust? Do I have an interest in keeping a gratitude practice or making changes to the one I have? Are there parts of me I don't fully embrace, like having strong legs? What might be small steps to loving myself more fully? What decisions lie ahead of me, and if I were to expand my choices from two to now ten or twenty, what expanded options would I include? How often do I ask others for advice before listening to my own heart? What practices might support my inner listening? How do I tend to my inner child, guide and love her/him, and learn from her/him? How am I also tender and kind to the adult in me? We all house a whole cast of characters inside of us like "The Purple Guy" described in this chapter. How would I describe the various characters/parts inside of me? What are wild, interesting, goofy, and beautiful experiences I might like to give myself? In my human imperfection, how do I still go forward and trust my voice?

Notes & doodling

A Miracle

Maybe the tomato plant shows me how to grow a miracle, inspiring me:

To know I need a foundation and plant my feet on this earth. Support my roots. Give myself kind friends. A warm blanket. Rest.

To know I need water and hydrate my life. Bathe in a spring shower. Drink plenty of water. Pause to really taste it. Keep a pitcher nearby. Know I am worth pouring into.

To know I need to soak in the sunlight. Sit in the outdoor seat. Look up at the sky.
Look in at my own fire. Make an appointment with Susanna Sunset. Applaud her.

Then be filled with expectancy for the fruition of fruit.

"All you need to grow a miracle is a little dirt, water, + sunlight."

Bless and Build Up

What if we used food to bless and build up? What if we said "I love you" with cinnamon and "I am proud of you" with pepper? Marshmallows mentioned your marvelousness and watermelon waxed on with well-wishing?

What if we kept running with this and stirred love into Thanksgiving dinner? Mashed gratitude into the potatoes for each person at the table? Basted the turkey with forgiveness? Dressed the salad with an oil of oneness?

These are the nutrients I would love to see listed on the side of my cereal box. At long last I would truly be full.

"I'm going to propose making sugar cookies with my parents because I would like more affirmations from them. I'll ask my mom to say her wishes for me as she stamps them & my dad to say his as he adds the sprinkles on top."

"These are not the ingredients my body needs now, but my soul does."

Above and Beyond

There are pronounced pockets of sorrow and celebration that move me to go above and beyond my simple fare.

I turn my attention to the bubbly, the milky, the volcanic aggregation of all that is scrumptious.

A cherry parfait with bubblegum bursts and coconut streams. An apple pie topped with cataclysmic caramel craters. Cocoa, espresso, and salt giving life to a triple layer cake, topped with vanilla cream.

There are so many layers to who I am and what I need and I am cooking up ways to most lovingly respond.

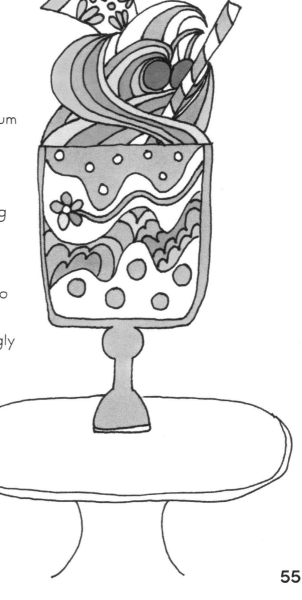

"I just want to stay in bed + read bad novels + eat raspberry–cream chocolates."

Permission Granted

I grant myself permission to delight in all I need in order to replenish.

Mystery and romance stories gift me with adventure and sweep me off my feet. They transport me to faraway lands from the comfort of my bed. Treats exist in tandem, as do fluffy pillows, deeper breaths, and a restful moon outside my window.

A day like this equips me to face the world again, feel more energized, and blaze forward with more brave steps.

Such pleasures are not really guilty ones at all, but instead, inspired and faithful.

Inviting

The tone of my voice
echoes the content of my
contemplation. The scent of
my body reveals the parameters of
my peace. The feel of my hug reveals the
hum of my heart. The taste of my cooking tells
the tale of my day. There are days I stir up fresh dill
and rosemary with golden potatoes
and luminous leeks, and do so with
open windows to hear birdsong
and rainfall and my own sweet
serenity. There are days I bake with
not enough chocolate chips
left in the bag, don't
take the time to
soften the butter,
and leave behind
the step to calm
and soften me.
I hear all of these
as earnest messengers, inviting
me to tend to what's cooking
within.

"my mom's cooking
tastes like
her deepest fears.
my aunt's kitchen
flows with love
+ is warm, spicy, +
delicious.
my friend's meals
are sage green
like her.
my food tastes
hesitant
because I'm afraid
my flavors
won't be appreciated."

" I want to buy beautiful dishes & eat the most colorful foods

The Spread on the Table

With pineapple-carved faces dressed in cranberry eyes, a strawberry mouth and carrot nose surprise, I set out to please my inner child with care, and pulled up a seat so she could be with me there.

I spread out our table with rainbows and queens, which appeared in the bowls and napkins and scene.

so I can please my inner child."

A train track surrounds this storybook meal, with cargo of broccoli and spinach and kale. It choo-choos in tofu and tilapia too, and teacups with flowers for me and for you.

I love her so much and wish her so well, so she knows she is queen of my heart and this tale. Her nutrition matters quite dearly to me, this love that I give in her vitamin C. I hope she will eat all I serve her like this, and feed her body like the royalty she is.

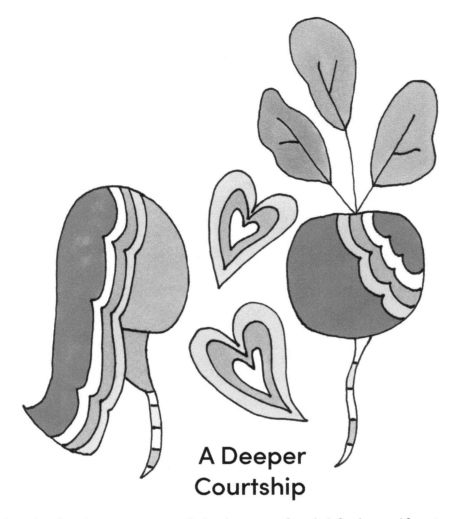

A Deeper Courtship

When I take the time to really look at my food, I find myself seeing more of what's there. Take the tomato, for instance. The outer red skin appears polished, glossy, glamorous. Its crown, a thick verdant star. Once it's sliced open, I see slippery seeds held in a glowy and jello-like glop. Thick milky lines run through inner rosy and mealy membranes. There is a symmetry to the inmost design, with the yellowy seeds and blonde middle mass working together to assemble a shining sun.

This getting-to-know-you stage isn't something to rush. It helps me to fall in love with the life that's in front of me. It helps me to desire a deeper courtship.

" I'm encouraging
myself
to eat
healthy food
by naming
my
encounters
a
'hot date'
with
a fig,
a tomato,
a radish. "

"I'm instructing myself to play with my food."

New Rules

I am freeing myself with new rules and ways to eat as the baton is passed from my parents' hands to mine, so that I can now wonderfully parent and please myself, as only I know how to do. I advise myself to play with my food. I display ingredients on a plate so they make the shape of a smiley face or a heart. I fill my bowl with a mishmash of color so I am sufficiently cheered. I have cooking adventures with delicious spices I didn't grow up with, like curry and coriander and mustard seeds. I generously share these fun foods with my friends.

This amended menu is delightful to digest, numinous with nutrients, chock-full of flavor, and jam-packed with delectable joy.

Relationship with food

Questions to row your boat with, to know and not (yet) know with. Questions to write your songs with, and closely walk your life with. Questions to tea party and book club with, and share or not (yet) share with. Questions to journal and meditate with, and lie down at angels' feet with. Questions only you know how to bring you best along with:

What self-care practices are life-giving for me/offer nourishing fruit? How can I remember to add extra loving ingredients when I am cooking for others, like taping the word "love" onto my salt shaker? Would that meal taste any different? What do I turn to when I need something that is extra scrumptious? What have I called guilty pleasures that I may instead cast in the light of being inspiring and faithful? How does the taste of my cooking reflect what's going on in my emotional life? How might I like to lovingly respond? How am I making and presenting my food so that it appeals to my inner child? What details do I observe when I take time to really look at my food, like the center of a tomato? What are rules about food in my upbringing that did and didn't serve me well? Are there any amendments that might better serve my joy?

Notes & doodling

three

Relationship
with
clothing

"My clothing
has
things to say,
like
'd care
how I put
my life
together'
&

'I am
here.'"

Selecting What Suits Me

I lay out what I will wear tomorrow with care on my bed. My soft retro dress that slips on like silky flower petals, sunshine polka dot leggings, bubblegum boots, and prized heart pendant and bangles.

Since I love and delight in each piece, I don't need to worry about colors or patterns matching. It is my merry love for each morsel that makes for the matching.

This process is as important as selecting all else that suits me, like kind friends, good food, meaningful vocation. Expressing who I am lives in the center of my selections. This is my fashion, my style, my glam, my runway.

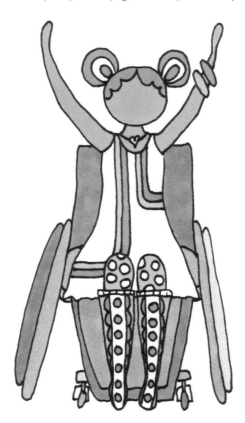

Fitting

I believe what my parents and grandparents and aunties and teachers tell me about myself. They are my mirrors and I absorb their reflection like lotion. Their view impacts how tall I walk and how much I hunch. Their words affect how I feel in my body and the fit of my clothes, and even greater, if I believe I fit in.

This is why words to a child of: "I love you just the way you are, I'm proud of you, You have what it takes, Your body is just right, I like being with you, I'm listening," are paramount.

And it's never too late to say them. New lotion can be applied. I select affirming people in my life and let in their kind words. I also parent myself and say to my life when I'm twenty and fifty and eighty, "I love you just the way you are." I watch the process of osmosis free me like Moses, parting waters inside me and making new land to stand on, so I can finally lay my claim that I really belong here.

"When I was
eight,
my grandma
told my mom
maybe I'd fit
into my clothes
if I didn't
eat
so
much."

Owning My Capacity

I am fashioned in the fabric of humanity. I am no better or worse than my sisters and brothers. I am capable of the most villainous acts I see in people as well as the s/heroic, and of all tender and tough tales told in between.

Knowing this ushers in a highway of hope. I notice the attributes I admire in others, and I can wonder where they also exist in me.

This capacity includes the green light to put together clothing in the creative ways I see featured in department windows and on precious people everywhere. Clothing of courage and kindness. Colors of an open heart and strong mind.

I align with the full spectrum of life and imagine the entirety of what is possible within me.

"I want her tunics & scarves that seem to protect her & her globe-like eyes & circular laughter. I want whatever invisible sword she's carrying that makes her unafraid."

"I'm going to haul out my spring wardrobe because I am tired of waking up in a stress suit.

Inhale and Exhale

I inhale the eye-catching inspiration of birds. The Red-Footed Booby. The Yellow-Billed Toucan. The Fiery Flamingo. The Pink-Headed Fruit Dove. The Green-Throated Hummingbird. The Blue Bird-of-Paradise.

I exhale tight and nude pantyhose. The black pencil skirt I can scarcely sit down in. The bleak boots. Any fripperies or frocks I am finished flocking to.

I will start my days in these clothes, sitting in my backyard patio with the beauty of the birds + a cup of tea."

I inhale my spring wardrobe. The sorbet-colored dresses. The necklaces with beads mimicking Jolly Rancher candies and multicolored marbles. The tennis shoes with tulips.

Then I pour a cup of tea and settle back into a life where I can preen my feathers and, at long last, sing again.

"Sometimes I take out my shoes & just look at the colors."

My Tall
Glass of Water

I am wild about nature shows and being transported into a state of awe and wonder, taking in the scope of life roaming vast lands and blue deeps. Take the Thorny Devil Lizard, for instance, who steps into a puddle following rare rains to soak water into every cell. The water can actually be seen moving up the body like a sponge, from spiky feet to pointy head.

This is what my rainbowlicious footwear dishes out for me. They are my tall glass of water. They hydrate from the feet up. They colorfully replenish, soaking joy into my cells and splendiferous sunshine into my smile.

The lizard of me needs such things, and I am tickled pink to provide.

Integration

I am integrating different parts of me into as many realms of my life as I can: listening to lovely music while I cook, playing cat's cradle with string with my friends as we talk, embroidering during a conference call.

Doodling in the classroom never needed to be grounds for trouble. It ought to qualify for extra credit.

Such integration helps me to be more whole. Plus it gives me more delightful-looking jeans.

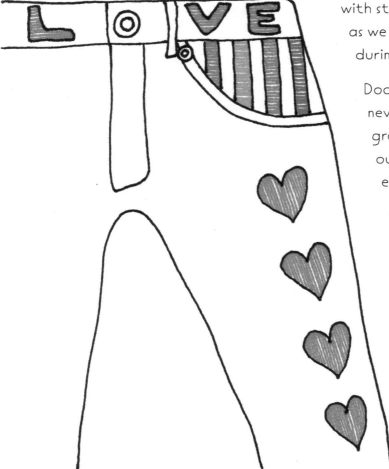

"I like to embroider during conference calls."

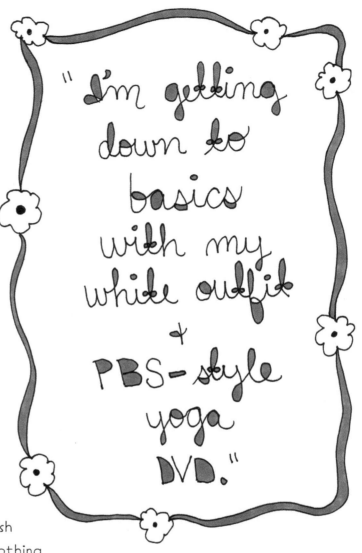

"I'm getting down to basics with my white outfit + PBS-style yoga DVD."

The Balance

As much as I love the commotion of colors and a vivacious vibe, I also cherish the balance of basics and nothing muchitude.

Clean white linens. A patternless pinafore. A soft smock. Music without words. A clear blue sky. Waving to the ocean waves within, communing with my waters and air.

I'm not unlike my laundry. I also need to treat both my colors and whites with consideration and care.

"It helps to remember
who I am
by looking back
at what I wore
as a little boy,
running around
in an unbuttoned
flannel shirt,
tender & free."

Wear a Life That Is Mine

My favorite childhood getup was my rainbow shirt and beige and purple polyester bell-bottom pants. My shopping cart included things like: Bazooka Bubble and Bubble Yum gum, Pop Rocks and Fun Dip candy, tins of Wild Cherry Lip Licking lip balm and sticks of Bonne Bell's Sour Grapes Lip Smackers. I collected marbles and rocks and played board games of Sorry! and Mr. Mouth. Hours of fun were spent with my Silly Putty, Slinky, and Spirograph. I was gaga for gifts of a Lite-Brite and View-Master. My Crissy Doll stood prominently, whose hair could be pulled long. The Carpenters and Bee Gees boomed on my record player and the Bionic Woman and Six Million Dollar Man saved the world on TV. I rode on my green bicycle with a banana seat down the block to my friend's house to play with her most excellent Easy-Bake Oven.

My early emergence reveals who I am with no edits or rewrites, reminding and exciting me to wear a life that is mine.

Relationship with clothing

Questions to row your boat with, to know and not (yet) know with. Questions to write your songs with, and closely walk your life with. Questions to tea party and book club with, and share or not (yet) share with. Questions to journal and meditate with, and lie down at angels' feet with. Questions only you know how to bring you best along with:

What would my outfit look like if I delighted in each piece? What are the textures, materials, colors, shades, patterns, lines, and layers? Are any words, hearts, polka dots, stripes, lace, scents, and sounds included? Do I prefer shiny or matte? What selections would my inner 5, 10, 15, 25, 50, future 100-year-old self merrily love? How do the words "I love you just the way you are" fit in with my clothing selections? What are memories of clothing/accessories I have seen in department store windows or worn by others I know and admire, and how might that be a personal invitation? What would I like to exhale that is stale from my closet, and what clothing would I like to inhale anew? What shoes hydrate me with joy from the feet up? Have I integrated my wears by knitting, embroidering, creative-endeavoring, alongside a TV show, a class, a phone call? Do I want to? What place do basics, neutrals, calming and quieting garments have in my life? What were my favorite toys, candies, music, movies, and clothing from my childhood? Do I recall how I had/have it in me to know what I love? How do these memories inform my current selections and precious life?

Notes & doodling

four

Relationship with animals

"I have a unicorn inside me + she points the way for me to go."

Inmost Magic

I have a unicorn inside my body. She helps me discern if it would be best to go this way or that way and helps me sort out how I am feeling. She shows me the stories I have stored up inside and compassionately guides me through the pages. She is a supreme and loyal friend, and I love her.

I seek her through stillness. I knock on her door with hush and quietude. She lives in a place of tender tiptoes. She must, in order to listen.

This is no small thing to be brave enough to approach her; to breathe myself into intermission from the activity of the day and be present to this unicorn. Yet I must persist if I am interested in my inmost magic, my middlemost me.

"If I can find beauty in my dog's moosey face, then maybe it's possible to detect the beauty in me."

Beauty

My dog has a moosey face. His muzzle is long enough to reach and rally my heart. His tall ears can hear the height of everything that's important, and his droopy bottom lip catches all that drops. His distinct markings on thick fluffy fur make him mine, and his milk chocolate eyes melt.

I see his beauty.

I have a humany face. A tall vertical line has formed in my skin between my eyes, showing people my years of squinting from sunlight and sensitivity to nearly everything. I have another line, this one wide and horizontal between my nose and mouth, appearing when I smile like a double rainbow of smiles. My once blonde and curly pig-tailed hair now manifests herself in black-and-white reels like old movies. Secret shrubbery can be sometimes seen inside my green eyes, harboring soft-hearted creatures like sheep and robust ones like elephants. My chin is punctuated with a mole that says, there, she is done.

I too see my beauty when I allow my wild eyes to open.

Thank You Note

Dearest Prozac Poodle,
Lexapro Labrador,
Celexa Corgi,

Thank you for knowing what I need, as you nudge and nuzzle your nose and full body against mine and take up residence, inviting me to stop everything and be still with you.

Thank you for being a First Call Responder when I weep and wail. Your everytime attendance and empathy eyes witness. Your weight warms. Your continuance comforts.

You daily reach and repair my heart, and I am forever changed and charged with gratitude. XOXOO, All of Us

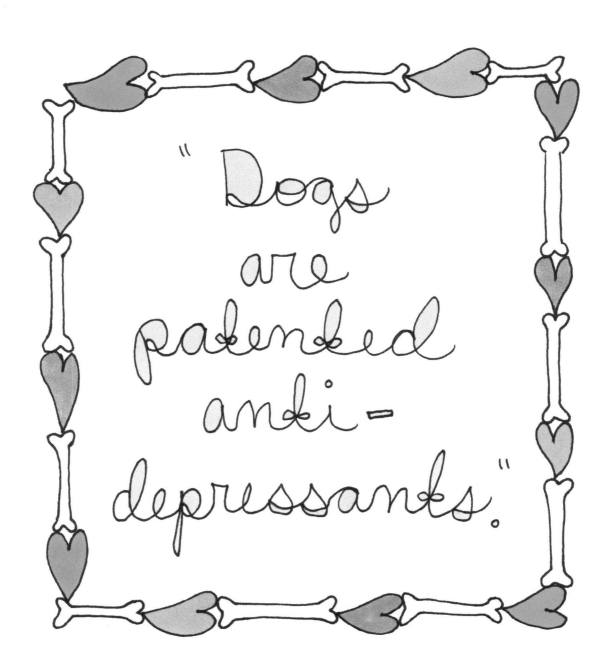

"Dogs are patented anti-depressants."

Take a Look Around

"I can't believe I got these answers wrong on the test. I knew them and blanked," I said to the tall giraffe. She responded, "Take a look around. Your life is always moving like the river. The test is just one twig of many, bubbling and burbling through your great life. If you would like, step into an inner tube and allow the waters to carry you downstream. Feel the flow. Connect with the current. Become one with the bigness." Next I said to the tall giraffe, "I spoke the most clumsy things at last night's gathering. I could just hear how off they sounded as they tumbled out," and she responded, "Take a look around. You can also find the word 'muscly' in the word 'clumsy' when you rearrange the letters. Last night's clumsy was your heart muscle revealing the vulnerability inherent in relationship with others. We all feel it. We just aren't all brave like you to keep stepping in." Then she knelt down and I climbed on her back. Together we rose up to the tree and grazed on her life-giving greens.

"I can see
my concerns
from a
new perspective
when I
stand tall
in the room
like a
giraffe."

" I breathed deeply to alchemize my stress into something beautiful + when I was ready.

A Better Vibe

I want to take time to care for my basic needs and use the method I've heard from others called "HALT," an acronym advising to halt and check if I am hungry, angry, lonely, and/or tired.

I know if I don't halt, check in, and care for my needs, I could cause harm to myself and others. I don't want to be like the bee and perish as I inject pain.

I saw my stress turn into a butterfly + I loosed that into the world."

I prefer the Monarch's method instead. I wish to soothe my hunger, anger, loneliness, and fatigue within the confines of my protective shell with: eating good food, listening to my feelings, considering compassionate company, and resting.

Once truly nourished, my oranges and blacks can break free and meet your greens and blues, and together build a better vibe for us all to fly in.

"Like the sloth, I'm moving methodically instead of from crisis to crisis."

My New Tune

I have found myself in praise of pause, yielding to yeast, breaking to breathe.

Allowing for stillness in between activity tames and tranquils me, stitching together my lost parts, scared parts, unintegrated parts.

Slothy Stillness has become my conductor and My Calmed Wholeness, my new tune.

It is then, with stable and steady steps, I can move from one branch to the next, and truly get to where I want to go.

"There are now three families of bluebirds in my yard

Best Friends Forever

I long for a Snow White life. To be best friends forever with the deer, tortoise, chipmunks, squirrels, raccoons, rabbits, and birds who surround her.

These adorable faces and magical helpers would be the cheeriest and chummiest of companions.

Maybe this yearning drops down even deeper. If this camaraderie were possible, it would imply that my feathered and furry friends

& it's as close to Snow White as I'm going to get."

and I would be thoroughly nourished. There would be no fear with full bellies. Peace and love would really reign.

There are moments of hopeful glimpses, when the curtain between cartoon and real life thins and life is agleam. Families of birds nest near. A friend stands at the door with a birthday cake. Dancers fill public spaces. Hearts with legs hold up "Free Hugs" signs.

Thus, this is my prayer. That we would all be fed with the nutrients we need, freeing me to go play with the fancy friends that our forest so generously gives.

"It felt calming to travel away from my perfeckionism in a submarine

Anemone and Me

Anemone wave their wild tentacles. Certainly I can unleash my messy mane too.

They are okay as they are. I am okay as I am.

Anemone dress in every color, from blazing blue to resplendent red. Certainly I can wear the rainbow too.

They are okay as they are. I am okay as I am.

*& go into
my deeper waters
where plants & animals
are okay just
as they
are. "*

Anemone range from a few centimeters in height to six feet long. Certainly I can accept ways I am both small and big too.

They are okay as they are. I am okay as I am.

Anemone protect the clownfish, and the clownfish polish the anemone. Certainly I can choose reciprocal relationships too, like with the unicorn, dog, giraffe, butterfly, sloth, and bluebird.

They are okay as they are. I am okay as I am.

Relationship with animals

Questions to row your boat with, to know and not (yet) know with. Questions to write your songs with, and closely walk your life with. Questions to tea party and book club with, and share or not (yet) share with. Questions to journal and meditate with, and lie down at angels' feet with. Questions only you know how to bring you best along with:

How do I approach my inmost unicorn, my muse, my magic? What helps me to listen to that internal place of wisdom? How would I describe the beauty of a beloved face of an animal in detail and how would I describe the beauty of my own? Perhaps I might write another page, in the form of a thank you note to an animal I adore. What situations am I feeling stuck and discouraged in? What might the tall perspective of a giraffe say to me about my concerns? Like the butterfly and sloth, who take the time to tend to what is within before emerging and moving, do I pause to hear if I am hungry, angry, lonely, and/or tired (HALT)? What have I noticed when I have and haven't done this? What are little steps I take to love myself and others, making it safer for birds to draw near? How might I rewrite or use the statement "Plants and animals are okay as they are and I am okay as I am" in my life? Could it be a mantra, meditation, creative writing prompt, invitation?

Notes & doodling

five

Relationship with humans / tension

If I Could Say Anything

This meal tastes terrible. I am bored with this conversation. I want to spend more time with you. I miss you. You hurt my feelings. I wish you would invite me. I wish you would call more often. I wish you would call less often, or not at all. I deserve better. I love you.

Hearing my uncensored sentiments doesn't mean I have to say them all out loud. I don't wish to bring about needless harm to others.

Hearing them does mean I will be more in touch with what's happening in my inner world, and by doing so, bring about the needed help for me.

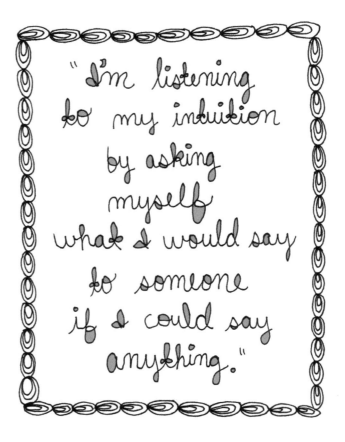

"I'm listening to my intuition by asking myself what I would say to someone if I could say anything."

"I've been watching female singers on YouTube. They stand up straight with chests open. When they close their eyes, it's like they are eating the most delicious ice cream. They are their own friend. Their own voices are their friends. I cry because I want to be that powerful."

To Be My Own Friend

It is an edifying, everlasting, and hard-won endeavor to be my own friend.

Being my own friend involves saying kind words to myself in the miserable midst of a friend not calling anymore, not getting the job I had hoped for, not feeling strong enough, smart enough, likable enough.

Being my own friend also involves saying kind words to myself in the merry midst of completing a quilt, cooking a brilliant meal with my first paella pan, acing an exam, feeling strong, smart, and likable.

It involves listening to myself as I journal, walk, meditate, and pray, and hearing myself as I talk to trusted friends and sing to myself in the shower.

It involves telling myself I am proud of who I am becoming and of who I am at this very moment, unconditionally and without exception.

I declare this hard-won friendship forming as no longer fleeting and fading, but instead, faithful and unflappable.

Even delicious.

Grief's Long Debut

Grief walks the earth of my body, with her long legs and stride,
pulling up green grassy growing things, as her feet drag from side
to side.

She takes up space galore and wilds her way with me, gusting
water through her blowhole and whaling endlessly.

She's in no haste or hurry, often staying a thousand suns, slumber
partying in the center of me, until her work is good and done.

I wish my friends' "How are you?" would match grief's long debut,
and return with intimate inquiry, for more than a day or two.

"My mom died five years ago & I wish people would still check in with me."

Collapses

To look without seeing, to eat without tasting, to hear without listening. I don't want a relationship devoid of presence.

I want our bellies to ache from so much laughter and crying that we collapse forward into one another.

I want to really feel something.

"I know I'm not in a real relationship when I'm in one + feel alone."

Reach Beyond

My language is as limited
as I perceive it to be, and
because of my preference
for the unencumbered,
I allow my walls to come
down and words to break free.

Communication can now reach beyond a
face-to-face conversation and text and email. My words
can fly to someone with the help of a wren's wing, and
a starry-eyed sonnet can swim to someone with the help
of a salmon. I can join my personal note alongside music
box notes and miraculously mail them all. Morse code
messages can tell my tales and syllables are sent off on
sailboats.

I can even type loving wishes to the world on my
keyboard and hand them to you with the help and the
heart of these paper airplaned pages.

" I'm having trouble
talking with my ex
+ am experimenting
with speaking
soul to soul
instead.
I open my music box
+ talk to him.
I also send him
morse code
messages. "

"When conflick is not resolving, I am practicing saying 'I am here with you'."

I Say, You Say

I say I need more time with you and you say you are giving all you can right now.

I am here with you.

You say you need me to help more around the house and I say but I just cleaned the whole kitchen yesterday.

I am here with you.

I say I need you to give me your full attention when I'm talking and you say you are.

I am here with you.

You say we ought to watch our pennies and I say pennies are for spending.

I am here with you.

I am here with you.

I am here with you.

"I speak softer to be heard."

Listen and Restore

I speak softer to be heard and say less words to say more. Then I join with you in silence, so we might listen and restore.

The old ways, I'm outgrowing, of bluster, boom, and roar. They've lost their seat at our table and lost their welcome at our door.

Two-Step

When I try to fix you, I trespass into your yard. These are your overgrown weeds and triumphant tulips to tend. Only you can know what they need, and they can only respond to you.

Besides, I rather relish working in my own secret garden, this place where I plant poems and posies and watch them grow up all wild and greenly like only I can.

When I try to support you, it takes the form of a wonderful visit and I look forward to your invitations. Maybe next time I can bring you some of my latest Zinnia seeds to share if you would like. Maybe you can share something with me too, like your expertise on how to best plant those amazing tulips.

I love how our own tendings make way for our gardens to grow like never before and for our two-step to become something we proudly applaud.

"It is not my job to fix, change, parent or raise. I want a partner, not a project."

Bring It All to the Chair

Did I say this just right? What did my words impress upon you today? How about all that I said last weekend? Was I understood? Do I look okay? Do you still like me?

I sit with myself and hear my vulnerability. I bring her to the chair and gently rock, backing and forthing with empathy. I say, I understand. I say, I like me. I say, I am just right. I say sounds like mmmm and ahhhh.

Then I reach for a soft blanket to cozy up with and open the windows for crickets and feathery music to find their way inside.

"I feel like my life depends on giving people the right impression of me."

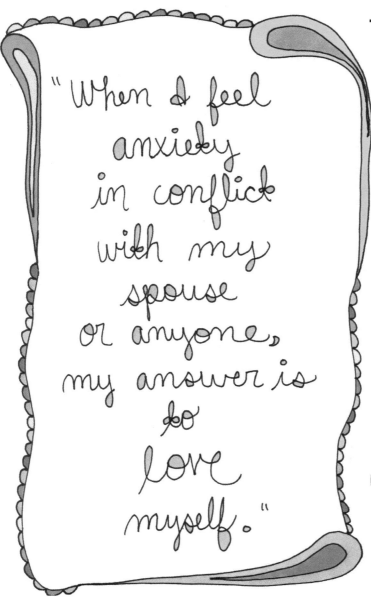

"When I feel anxiety in conflict with my spouse or anyone, my answer is to love myself."

Through and Through

I stand here with my heart, in all my swirls and hues, promising through thick and thin to love me through and through.

When I face the tension arising in me and you, I'll take that time to love myself and make my promise true.

When I feel the tear between my inner views, I'll extend my love to both my halves and let that be my glue.

My love will be the gift, my eternal avenue, to move ahead with a heart more whole, and more equipped to love you too.

Relationship with humans/tension

Questions to row your boat with, to know and not (yet) know with. Questions to write your songs with, and closely walk your life with. Questions to tea party and book club with, and share or not (yet) share with. Questions to journal and meditate with, and lie down at angels' feet with. Questions only you know how to bring you best along with:

What would I say to someone I hold tension with if I could say anything? In my private moment of doing this, what does this allow me to hear? What is the hard work I am doing and might consider doing to be my own friend? How might I consider being a friend to myself and others who are grieving and vulnerable, as well as showing up in the places of delight? Do I feel alone when I'm with others and/or lovingly accompanied? How might I creatively consider ways to respond when communication feels difficult, like joining my personal note alongside music box notes from afar, and saying "I am here with you" when near? How do I adjust my volume in order to be heard? What place does softness and silence have? How do I try to fix or support someone else's garden and how do I tend to my own? How am I lovingly present to myself when I am wondering what other people think of me? How do I extend this same love to myself when I am in conflict with others?

Notes & doodling

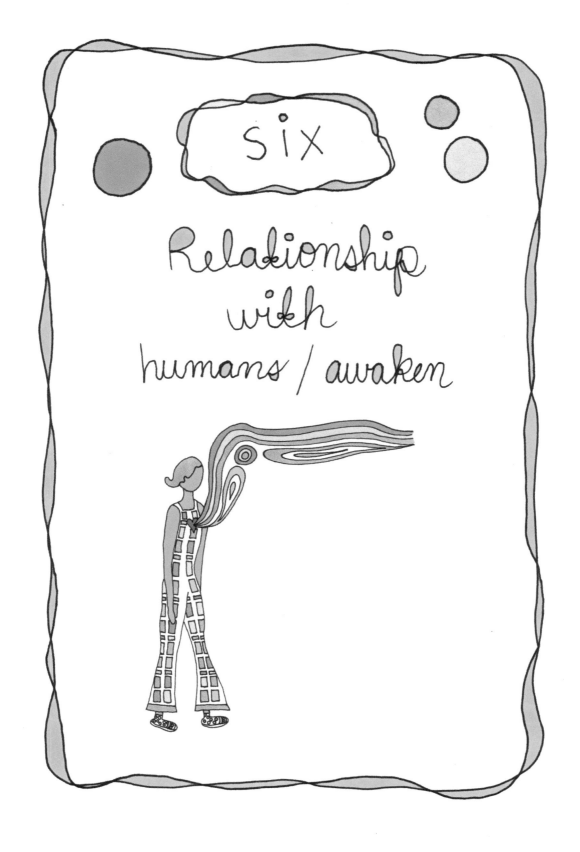

six

Relationship with humans / awaken

"Romantically I'm turning into the person I'm proud to be

A House of Wholeness

I used to keep part of my heart hidden away in the house of hesitation. I would mostly allow myself only the nicest of expressions, like saying how much I appreciated this and how much I appreciated that, and responding with only how happy I felt. While that was true yang, I didn't share my more vulnerable yin.

because
of not taking
a super long
time
to share my
vulnerability."

A U-Haul is now at my door to haul-all-of-U into the house of wholeness. This is a new place where I can also allow myself the bravest of expressions, like saying how much I appreciate this and how I am also hurt by that, and responding with how happy and how melancholic I am feeling, and not needing to wait a super long time to say so.

My yin and my yang are finding the furniture here to be far more comfortable and are scheming to spread out and stay a while.

"I need to
own up
to the way I
hurt her.
I don't need to be
upset with myself
because
I'm not making this
about being
good or bad.
It's a
responsibility thing."

A Responsibility Thing

My words to you emerge out of my heart with pointy edges and hurried writing, the way I might fill in answers in the last thirty seconds of a timed test when I'm running behind.

I can feel the letters blaze through my throat and set fire to my lips as they find their way out. My body has been here before. She recognizes the flame.

They dart directly to you and harm you with their heat.

I have built stones in a circle to contain the fire. I have spent hours on the beach lifting up the heavy boulders, but it never works. Fire is a wild thing. It is her nature to draw outside the lines. It is her way to crackle, fly, and burn.

Since fire can't thrive without furious air, I do the one thing that only I can do. I stay with myself. I breathe in calm and I breathe out compassion. I allow the hot words to softly ember into silence.

I then come to you and say I am sorry. I take responsibility. I stay with my restful breathing. I stay with my kindness. I stay with you. I stay with me.

Slowly now. Breathing, breathing. Gentle pinks now. Breathing, breathing. I am sorry now. Breathing, breathing. I am sorry.

"We each closed our eyes & the traumatized child in me waved to the traumatized child in him

Youfully and Mefully

Encountering the child in me and the child in you has changed things.

It seems to have opened my eyes to see more clearly what is within and all around.

The yellows never looked so yellow. The May flowers never smelled so May-flowery.

& when our eyes reopened, I saw my flowers & wondered if they had always been so yellow."

I rush to the yard and relieve the raspberry bushes of their generous growth, filling our eager hands with fruit. The raspberries never tasted so raspberry.

You never looked so youfully and I never looked so mefully.

Truth and Realness

What are you afraid of when you walk into the dark cave of your imagination? What might be around the corner when you are alone in the house and hear an unexpected noise?

What moves you into miraculous merriment when you walk into the rainbow room of your imagination? What is finally happening here that has made you so happy?

If these questions are interesting to you, then you have my full attention.

"I used to be intrigued by not knowing everything about a person but I don't want mystery anymore. I want truth & realness."

"I am highly sensitive & intuitive & pick up on people's states & needs, but it doesn't mean I'm responsible to take care of those needs."

Highly Sensitive

I don't have much skin, and sensations all around me get all the way in.

I hear your tone like the drop of a pin, then the turn of your cheek, then the twitch of your chin.

I see the mountain as it trembles in you, but I cannot climb it. I mustn't. It's true.

This is your journey to tend and your journey alone, from the stories of your skin to the marrow of your bone.

I send you my love and return my gaze to my center, to hear my own voice and with reverence, re-enter.

Now and Then

Back then, my dad moved far
away and didn't spend enough time
with me.

Forward now, I move in closer to be present
to my stories. I send love and empathy to all the
beauty and breaking inside,

making room for relationships with a balanced presence.

The rest I must release.

Back then, my mom moved in too close and spent too
much time needing me.

Forward now, I move in with compassionate distance to
be present to my stories. I send breath and spaciousness
to all the beauty and breaking inside,

making room for relationships with a balanced presence.

The rest I must release.

"Because
of him,
I worked
on
myself
+
because
of the
work,
I had to
let him go."

"I broke up with him but not with my worth."

Worth

A moon of mourning fills my belly and stars shine light on my sorrow/I am worth all the moons and stars.

Noah's Ark has flooded in and tears fill my eyes/I am the apple of my eye.

The unknitting knocks me over and I fall to my knees/I am the bee's knees.

You aren't here/I am.

Golden Hours

I recall and hold dear
the grade school note
from a boy asking "Do you like
me?" These were the golden hours
of learning love's ABC's.

I wish to return to the flutter and
giggle and bashful smile across the
room. I now lean into the
memory of the
sun casting a
shadow on his
face, wonderfully
lighting the eye that
was looking at me.

Why did I think this was something to
outgrow? How did I miss this instruction
was for life? The sun coming through is
an eternal thing, and I'm walking into it
with my heart open wide.

"I want to leave behind men who hem & haw & instead, have a relationship with someone who stupid loves me."

and wish them well

"If someone doesn't care about your life, jettison them."

and wish them well

and wish them well

and wish them well

and wish them well

I Am Ready

Farewell, Not Calling after
Surgery. Goodbye, Delivering
Donuts When You Know
I'm Trying to Eat Healthy.
Cheerio, No Time for Me.
Adieu, You and You and You.

Welcome, Listening to Me
as I Cry. Hello, Making Soups
for Our Families Side by Side.
Good day, Calling to Say Happy
Birthday. True blue, You and You
and You.

And, this is also about Me and
Me and Me.

I release the ways I don't care for
myself with a colorful chute. I fasten
a harness around Not Nourishing
Myself Well and Not Taking Time to Listen
to My Heart and send them out of my
airplane with love.

I embrace the ways I care for myself with providing first-class seats to
Speaking Kind Words to Myself and Asking Myself How I Am and serve them
warm towels and pretty meals.

I have a life of ascension to live, and I am ready to rise.

Suitable for a Queen

Your walk is wisdom, your words are well done, your garden is kindness, and your garments are fun.

Your heart is a miracle with rainbows running through, carrying the gentlest of greens and the most benevolent blue.

Your crown is empathy, compassion, and care, and this is the outfit matching the one that I wear.

" Queens
need to know
their
worth
+ find
their
Kings. "

"I can both
love her &
not need
to settle.
Something
around the corner
is
bigger & better –
even if
in solitude."

A House of Paradise

In solitude, I hear crickets in summer, leaves crunch under foot in fall, heaps of snow fall from the roof and thump to the earth in winter, and birdsong in spring.

In stillness, I am with my breath. I sit by the water. The sun speaks to me in light. I watch the ducks paddle by, leaving gentle swirling water behind them.

I don't mean to say pain isn't in this place. It's just that I treat her well. I bring her tea. I listen. I love.

I live in a house of paradise.

In the soft music of my words, this is what I'm saying to you: I will answer your knock if you house paradise too.

"I won't just choose a person to be with. I'll choose the story."

The Story

I head to the library and pile books on the table, loading up fantasies, fairies, and fables.

I read stories of plunging to the depths of despair, then rising back out with wilderness hair.

There are pages of castles, oceans, and trees, of magic carpets, bright lights, and the art of trapeze.

I turn to chapters of green lands and kind people, with food for them all and humble church steeples.

These are the places where my heart can break free, and these are the stories where I'll find you and me.

Benefits of Growing

Bamboo plants make a mess with their leaves flying through the air. Azaleas and cherry trees drop all their flowers. Acacia shrubs have sap and pods, and winds find them too and blow their sticky blooms about.

This same messy life is a prolific life.

Bamboo plants grow quickly and spread profusely. Azaleas can live for decades. Some of the flowering cherry trees also produce edible fruit. Acacia's stems aren't just blooming at the tips but also sprouting along the sides.

This life is my life too.

When I do my work in relationships and especially out of the messy places, saying soft and brave words and repairing my own roots, my foliage family promises one sure thing: growth will become a wild and hearty thing, and I sure as sunshine am going to show up for it.

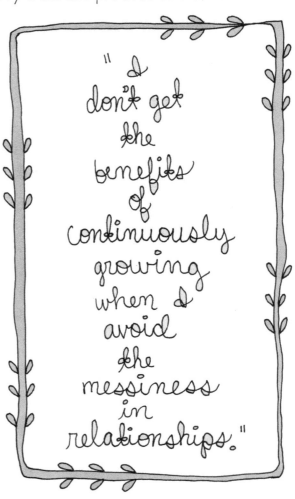

"I don't get the benefits of continuously growing when I avoid the messiness in relationships."

Relationship with humans/awaken

Questions to row your boat with, to know and not (yet) know with. Questions to write your songs with, and closely walk your life with. Questions to tea party and book club with, and share or not (yet) share with. Questions to journal and meditate with, and lie down at angels' feet with. Questions only you know how to bring you best along with:

When it is safe to do so, how am I expressing both what I appreciate/am supported by and what I need/am hurt by in my relationships? Am I able to compassionately stay with both myself and another person when I take responsibility and say I am sorry? What do I notice when I consider the inner child within others and within myself? What are some questions I might ask a loved one if I wanted truth and realness? What might I also share of my own truth and realness? How can I lovingly listen to someone else's feelings and yet not take them on as my own? What has been too little or too much in my relationships? What would feel just right? What needs releasing and embracing? Can I see my worth as unconditional and remaining, no matter who stays or leaves in my life? Am I letting love in that is wholehearted? Am I letting love in that is suited for a queen/a king? Am I opening my paradise-door for a paradise-visitant? What story do I want to select? Do I stick around long enough to receive the benefits of growing through the messiness of valued relationships?

Notes & doodling

Seven

Relationship with humans / embrace

AMAZING EYES

"He doesn't like the Beatles but I can forgive him because of his amazing eyes."

His Eyes

Waves and whales in his ocean blue, with salt and sand and starfish too. Teeming krill and manatee, joined by sea horse company. So much life in this sapphire sea, where I'm in real deep and happy to be.

"I'll always remember my first ~~boyfriend~~ gave me perfume & Hostess Ding Dongs."

Gifts

Big gifts are often little, like a 100 Grand candy bar, a rock, a marble.

The swirls in them say things like: I've been listening to you, I understand you, I've been thinking about you, my heart is open to you, and I love you.

Even though eaten, misplaced, or tucked away, the messages will endure like Willy Wonka's Everlasting Gobstopper, and I am forever grateful for them.

My Shining Stars

You are the ones I can tell all my stories to/Crinkled up, wrinkled up, vulnerable me.

You are the ones I can wear my pajamas with/Pink-plaid, giraffe-printed, polyester me.

You are the ones I can walk through humdrum with/Wordless, breathing, needing arm-in-arm me.

You shine a light I can be in the night with/Loyal, luminous, celestial you.

"I know the people I can share me with & I call them my shining stars."

"I'm making space for pen pals."

Pen Pals

I wish to make space again for the handwritten letter. The kind where I can recognize someone by the way they write their letter "a" and by how small or sweeping their script is.

I remember my own stationery from childhood. Holly Hobbie and Betsey Clark girls were drawn on pastel papers. Snoopy and Garfield brightened others. Envelopes were sealed with sticker-taped words and strawberry-scented scratch-and-sniff stickers, and the first letter of my name was stamped into colorful wax.

When did I decide that growing up meant replacing mail that smells like sweetest fruits from the forest for ads and bills? Dear Best Friend Forever, please don't delay and write back soon!

" my mom told me, in her last days, it made her feel so much better to look into my eyes."

My Ultimate Reverie

My relationships are my ultimate reverie, and my hope is to someday rest into a soft pillow and blanket that have been filled with the feathers of friendship.

I will wonder if my words have been kind enough, if I have conveyed enough empathy, listened enough, was present enough. I will hope to forgive myself generously for when I have fallen short and feel a peace wash over me for the moments my love has found a way forward.

My ending will be a nod to my beginning, when nearby loved ones searched for my ten fingers and toes. Only later it is I who will be doing the looking, for a beloved hand to hold and essential eyes to gaze into, and it is all that will matter.

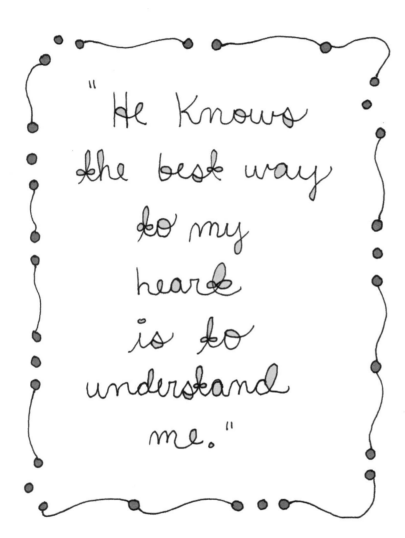

"He knows the best way to my heart is to understand me."

The Keys

Here lies the key to my heart: Lean in to understand me.

Here lies the key to my whole universe: Be someone who values understanding.

Here lies the key to understanding me: Listen.

Here lies the key to connecting with me: Tell me what you heard me say.

Then the door will unlock and swing open as we both do the hard and wonderful work with these keys held in our hand-in-hands.

Naming

I am named as I enter this world
and this marks my arrival, the
beginning of being known, and a sense
of belonging with those who are naming me.

New witnesses whisper new namings as I grow older. They
sometimes offer the slightest of alterations and at other
times, a whole new name: Sweet Special, Spring, Sunshine,
Cranberry Queen.

When this occurs and the naming carries resounding
resonance, then I know beyond a shadow of a doubt, you are
a diamond in my dynasty.

"When we were dating, he called me his Cranberry Queen & I called him my Pauper Prince."

Having Fun Together

The young part of me, with an innocence that shines bright like light on a morning lake, knows how to draw near to people.

This part of me knows to join my friend under her piano and play with our stuffed animals, to play our 45 vinyl records and sing our hearts out, and to race into the middle of a great mystery together in the enchanted forest of my back yard.

The grown part of me, with a wisdom that shines bright like a lantern on an evening walk, knows now to take her lead.

My Relational Nature

I embrace my relational nature and lean into the creatures who simply show me to me. They give wide open space for me to bring my authentic life forward.

They observe the obvious of me with love: the peanut butter I mix into my cereal, the writing I turn to in the morning, the way the lines in my face move as I smile, the rainbows threading through all of my wears.

These are the relationships that help bring me home. With the secure grounding that comes from someone lovingly seeing my distinct essence, I am ironically freed to take flight with open arms and launch into all that's calling me.

"I was told my husband & I had multiple lives together & in one life, we were the same person."

Spiraled

My DNA is spiraled into yours and yours is spiraled into mine, an inherited, color-coded, cellular design.

Our paths are interwoven and our stories intertwined, for where I find your heartbeat, I most certainly find mine.

We are two lights and yet somehow are one, as we walk through this world, you the moon, me the sun.

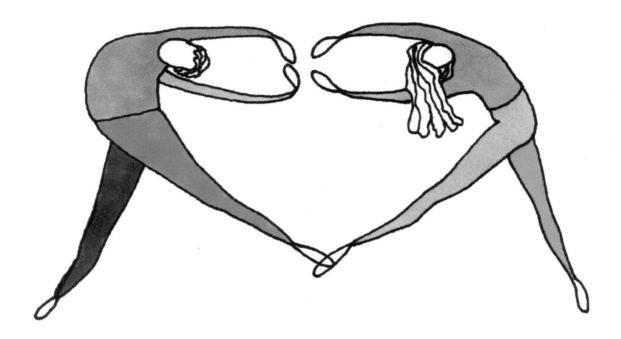

Like a Poem

Let's sit in a meadow and breathe, in the daisies and breeze, become one with the great growing greens, tall as the grasses and trees.

Let's rise from this place and dance, in the delicacy of a spring shower, joining music of feathery wings, flying beside us in their soft power.

Let's rest in the sound of singing bowls, in the billowing bed of the night, surrendering all words and willings, tranquiling us into twilight.

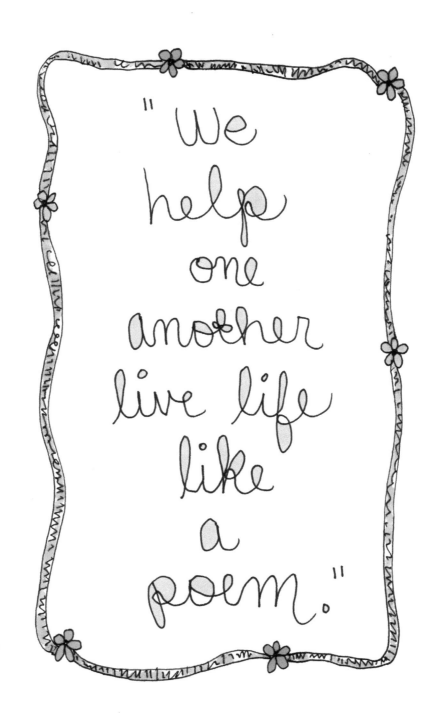

"We help one another live life like a poem."

"I am
wrapped
in her
soul
&
she is
wrapped
in mine."

Soul-Wrapped

There exist these swirling and
whirling times when we connect
with one another on a soul level.

At such a moment, perhaps there is a
groovy supersonic charge rippling through
time and space, dressed in lightning whites
and aurora borealis greens.

Colors hurtle through space and find us,
leaving us speaking the same words at
the same moment, singing the same song,
and eating from the same apple.

It is no small thing to swim in such a current. It is
no small thing to let love connect us all.

> " Each of us
> is being
> who we are
> with
> each other
> &
> that's where
> all
> the
> good stuff
> is. "

Who We Are

The stars are magnets and pull my eyes upward, considering what's beautiful, and I bring my ideas back down to the ground to be seen.

Gravity pulls your eyes downward and you comb the rocks, considering what's beautiful, and you raise your finds into the air to be seen.

Being awake to the intricate stories in my kaleidoscopic soul, my constantly moving Technicolor triangles and trapezoids, is as important as breathing, and having the great honor of looking through yours too helps me to see more of the whole world. Thank you.

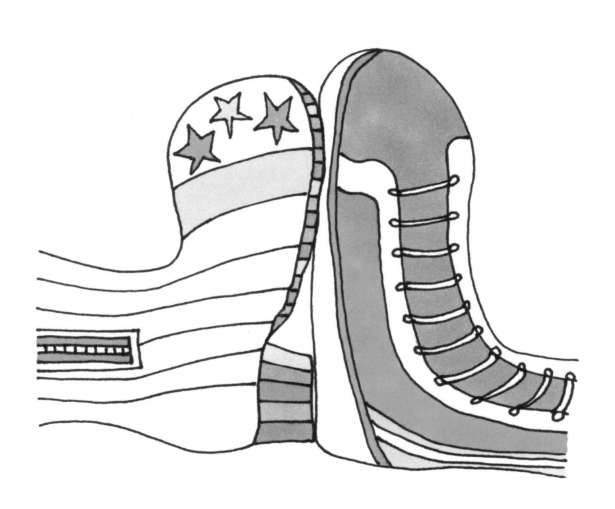

189

Relationship with humans/embrace

Questions to row your boat with, to know and not (yet) know with. Questions to write your songs with, and closely walk your life with. Questions to tea party and book club with, and share or not (yet) share with. Questions to journal and meditate with, and lie down at angels' feet with. Questions only you know how to bring you best along with:

What do I adore so much in another person that makes it okay to not have everything in common? What have been my favorite gifts from a love? Who is someone/people I would call my shining star(s)? How do I recognize a shining star in my life? Would I like to make space again for the handwritten letter on pleasing stationery? Who might be my pen pal? Whose hands will I hope to hold in my last days and how do I hold them now? How do I listen to and understand others, and how am I likewise heard and understood? What names do people have for me and how do I feel about them? Do I have any special names for them? Do I make space for fun in my relationships? Which relationships most closely reflect my distinct essence and leave me feeling I can launch into the world being more freely me? What are my thoughts about how I can be one with another human being and/or two? What would it mean to me to live life like a poem alongside another? What do I think of the words "being soul-wrapped" with another person? Am I in relationships where we are being who we are with each other? What is the good stuff?

Notes & doodling

eight

Relationship with community

Inherently Interdependent

Quantum mechanics looks at our very foundation and shows us how electrons only exist when in interaction. We see this same principle at work when we zoom the camera out wider, viewing our distinct nature when in relationship. I learn immeasurably more about a dog when I see one relate to a human being than when I watch the dog alone. Life is inherently interdependent, and when touched by another, more fully awakens.

I know this from how I respond to being touched by love. After time with my tribe, something gets stirred. I want to exercise again, pick up the guitar, cook new recipes, and ride a fire-breathing dragon into the sunset.

Maybe this interaction, when done lovingly, provides me with some kind of mirror reflection. I hear my name being called and I come to life. I become a real "boy," like Pinocchio, only I go forward and live the bigger truth of me.

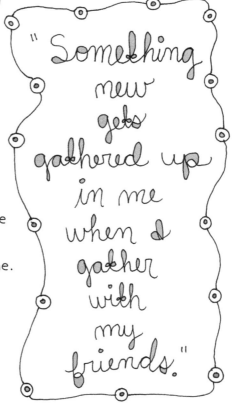

"Something new gets gathered up in me when I gather with my friends."

The Shape of a Heart

Dearest darling neighbors, I thank you for the ways, you've lent an ear, a hug, a bloom, and lit my dimmer days.

Your love has made our block, a straight line from the start, with all your care and kindness, the shape of a heart.

How can I thank you, for taking care of me? I'll start with these few words, and plant an apple tree.

"I call my neighbors my Kneebors because they have held me up when I have been on my Knees."

FLOWERS

"& buy flowers from a nearby jail."

FLOWERS

How Can It Be?

How can it be that a tree can grow through a stone wall and grass rise up through a concrete sidewalk? How can it be that flowers can emerge from a prison?

How can it be that love can grow through my defended heart?

Trees and grass and flowers and love are supple and strong enough to spring through the hardest of surfaces.

Infinitely wise are the living things, and so very brave.

"we might all have quirks & peccadilloes but underneath we are all so similar. we all speak of

Tuning In

It helps to know that you and I are more similar than we are different.

You don't want to be overlooked in the room any more than I do, so I will look into your eyes.

love being
felt in our
hearts.
Rarely do
people tell
you they love
you with all
their knees."

You don't want to be silenced any more than I do, so I will lean in and listen.

You don't want empty affection any more than I do, so I will express a love that is genuine.

What might happen if we all tuned into this telephone line? Might we finally reach one another?

Becoming a Warrior

Breathe in, two three four, out, two three four.

Calm in, two three four, out, two three four.

Have no fight left in, two three four, out, two three four.

Welcoming this warrior in, two three four, out, true free restore.

"I'm teaching my students & myself that the key to becoming a warrior is to practice calm."

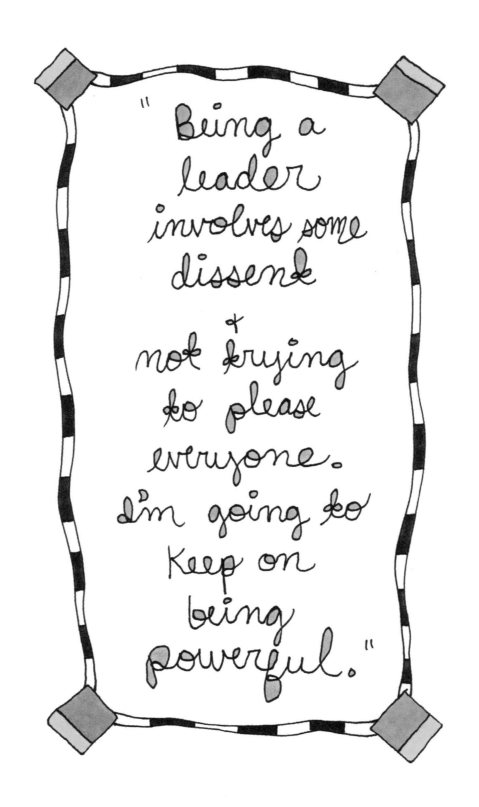

"Being a leader involves some dissent & not trying to please everyone. I'm going to keep on being powerful."

Being a Leader

Here I stand, with the clothing
I wear, bright colors, mixed
patterns, righteous ribbons in hair.

Here I speak, with words
unwrapping for you, of love
clucks and peace trucks, and olive
branches too.

Here I shine, in the light of the day,
being who I am, giving no power
away.

You might love me for this, or you
might well be done. Either way, I
am here. I am facing the sun.

I'll trust the rhapsody, in this
rhythm I'm livin', as I honor the
gift, to play all I've been given.

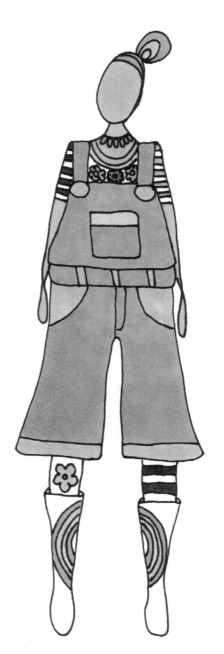

When Joined

I look out my window and watch the snow fall, each flake a meticulous masterpiece, and when joined by trillions, they together make possible the laughter of children as they stick a carrot in a snowman's face, create needed ground for the majestic march of the polar bear, and make the peaks of our tallest mountains shine like diamonds.

"If I could run the world, I wouldn't do it alone. I'd do it with circles of women."

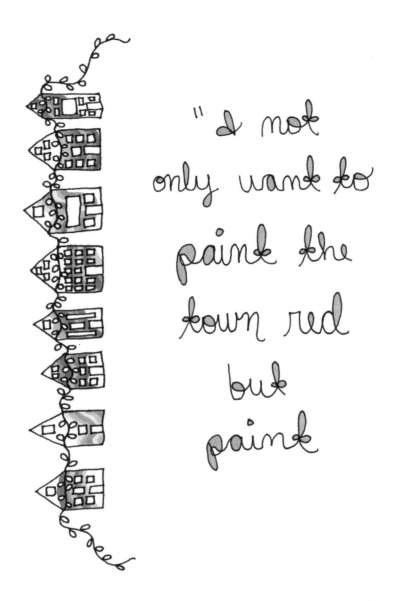

"I not only want to paint the town red but paint

This Whole Avenue

I love the house of red, with a goat and chicken farmstead. I love the house of orange, with unique residents who don't rhyme with anything. I love the house of yellow, filled with gentle fellows. I love the house of green, with cooking smells

with
every color,
celebrating
connection with
all
people."

from Bernadine and Pauline. I love the house of blue, with a multigenerational crew. I love the house of purplish-pink, with children selling their classic lemonade drink.

I love this whole avenue, living colors of you and you and you.

Relationship with community

Questions to row your boat with, to know and not (yet) know with. Questions to write your songs with, and closely walk your life with. Questions to tea party and book club with, and share or not (yet) share with. Questions to journal and meditate with, and lie down at angels' feet with. Questions only you know how to bring you best along with:

What do I notice happening with me following time with people I care about and who care about me? What awakens? What are my relationships like with my neighbors? Where are surprising and unlikely places I have found lovely people? What memories occur to me when I think of times love has emerged out of my defended heart? What is my experience with being seen, heard, and loved, and how do I offer this to others? How might being a calm warrior help both me and my community? In what ways do I get caught up with trying to please everyone and in what ways do I stand in my authentic power? In what ways have I joined with others (or might like to) to create a greater music, harmony, offering? What are the collection of relationships and neighborhoods, landscapes and animals, cultures and clothing I see all around me? How might I greet and serve and honor them?

Notes & doodling

"I awake with songs in my head that the angel DJ's gave me."

Between Destinations

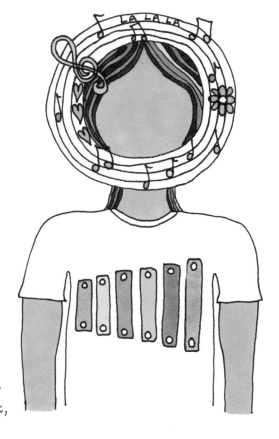

There are these in-between moments, liminal twinklings in time, when I can kneel down and gather up glittery sand from the beach of my soul.

These are the hours I am neither here nor there, as I first awaken but yet not fully, and as I drive, daydream, walk, swim, shower.

It is in these between destinations-places where I come to know something needed and new. I can recall my dreams, the perfect gift presents itself, the next poem is written. Countless times I have emerged from the restroom with the words "I was just thinking . . ."

Sometimes songs will drop in with tremendous reassurance, comfort, and care. The veil can become so thin that I can almost see the notes spilling in straight from angel's hands.

All That I Am

I overflow with light. I walk with weightless feet through fields of sunflowers. I keep rainbows for pets. I extend kindness and I want to.

I swim in shadows and movement is effortful. Lethargic petals wave through my waters. I get tangled in seaweed. I speak spiky-coral words, even though I don't want to.

It's easy to love myself just when I shine, but I'm an earth angel and need to love the whole of my hemispheres all of the time.

"I might have a halo but it's crooked & tarnished."

"I meet quarterly with a group of women & we work on our soul journals."

What Would Happen?

What would happen if I began a soul journal and reflected on the following questions: What am I grateful for? What do I dream of? What brings me joy? What is my body needing from me? What are spiritual practices I feel drawn to, that might help deepen a connection with my heart and with the heart of the universe/nature/ God? What does my soul want me to understand? What are ways I can raise my vibration?

What would happen if I joined a group of other dear souls, who valued these same questions, and we worked on our journals together?

What if all pens, pencils, magic markers, crayons, stickers, paints, scissors, and glue sticks were available? What if we could all express our responses safely? What if we all held each other in love?

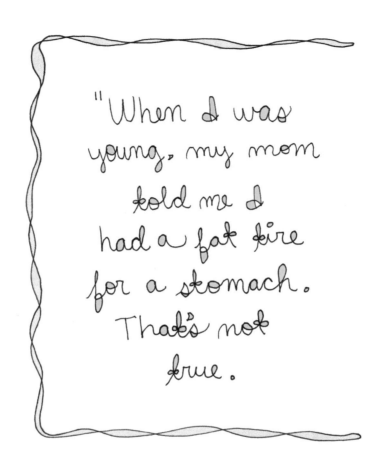

"When I was young, my mom told me I had a fat fire for a stomach. That's not true.

My Body

I house a colorful gumball machine filled with: love, chakras, light, stories, breath, memories, tears, laughter, hugs, words, voice, poetry, music, and worlds of moreness.

The flavors are mystically mind-bending, and colors soulfully swirling.

There are extra prizes included amid these round, chewy pleasures, much like I might find in a Cracker Jack

caramel-coated popcorn bag or in my Cap'n Crunch cereal box. Newly found constellations and other surprises that even I don't know to anticipate are nestled in there.

This gumball residence has no groove for quarters. My spheres of love and light and breath cannot be bought, bartered, or bribed. This beautiful blend is a holy one and can only be freely given.

And you will only see me when you look deeply through your own gumball-eyes.

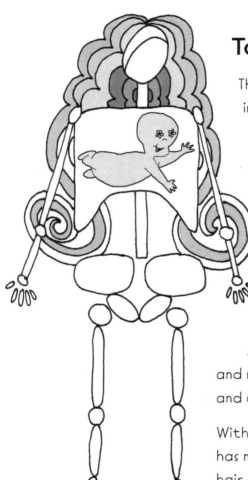

To Be Healed

The winds are rushing the rain sideways into my west-facing windows. The porch chairs have fallen over again.

The winds become restless with barriers. They want to blow in.

I'm not settled either and take a chance, opening my windows and doors, my arms and my palms, my heart and my lungs, my worries, my stories.

Air gusts through my house, spiraling and rolling her way through dusty rooms and old piles, whistling all the way.

With the same flurry she arrived with, she has now left and the house falls silent. My hair drops down. I exquisitely exhale.

I am ready to be healed. For the knocking over of everything.

"I'm paying attention
to what heals me
by hanging art on
my walls
+ wearing clothes
that feel like
kindness + love.
It's like
Casper the friendly ghost
is going through
all the holes
in my bones."

"I'm so much ~~better~~ as a mom + wife + person when I let my soul shine through. It's been contained in an

Great Big Ball of Soul-Sunshine

I embody the most astonishing of contents, with a great big ball of soul-sunshine and large lung-breathbeams inside.

My light is as real as my breath, glowing inside through the chemical reactions of elementary photon particles. We see this in fireflies, jellyfish, squid, and glow-worms. Sensitive cameras reveal a rhythmic glow that brightens and fades over the course of the day.

iron box because I convinced myself that I didn't have time to release it & that it didn't matter,"

This blaze bursts into fireworks beyond my body and fills our atmosphere with floral auras and extrasensory energy. It's all peace and love, baby.

I don't want to lock down this light any more than I want to block my breath. I wholeheartedly wish to live and to do so vibrantly.

I want to pray poems and swim in sunsets and plan laughter potlucks. I want to soak up and feel all the words and waves and wow, and perhaps more than anything, I want to become this offering.

"I'm trusting
the
divine detours
in my life
because
they have formed
the woman
I am
becoming
& I like
who I am."

Divine Detours

All that comes my way is a doorway into my becoming. Beloveds dying and departing. Not getting into graduate school right away. A worldwide pandemic penning me in.

I resist it all and wrestle with the best of them. My heart is heavy, thunky, mad. I grieve with my lip hanging low and feet lifting layers of earth with them as I stomp.

My feet also turn up treasure. Wild flowers and clover wind their way in between my toes, and hearty roots and vines from those prolific pumpkins.

I come alive more vibrantly and vow to not leave my side. I take a new job until I get into school and because of it, find one of my finest friends. At home at length, I finally write this love letter to you and let my natural and wild hair colors have their way.

These detours aren't easy, and still I would walk through a thousand more fires to burst brightly into my best blossom of me.

"The warm arm
of Mercy
is around me,
leading me forward
with
softness & kindness,
appearing
in lavender & pink,
& shimmering inside
with a
silver & gold
glow."

The Same Letters

When I get really, really silent and listen, I realize I am in good company (silent and listen have the same letters).

As near as my breath, birds sing the song of life. A few steps away, neighbors are waking up their dreaming children and pouring eggs into frying pans. My inner child and purple guy and gypsy are always caravanning with me. I can say to myself "I love you just the way you are" and choose beloveds I can say "I am here with you" with. There are extra-special days when everything is coming up roses and I can glean the angel who has her arm wrapped right around me (glean and angel have the same letters).

I am great with gratitude for having the eyes to see my revered relationships and to know that they see me too (the eyes and they see have the same letters).

Relationship with divinity

Questions to row your boat with, to know and not (yet) know with. Questions to write your songs with, and closely walk your life with. Questions to tea party and book club with, and share or not (yet) share with. Questions to journal and meditate with, and lie down at angels' feet with. Questions only you know how to bring you best along with:

What new insights occur to me when I am between destinations? (Between sleep and awake states, daydreaming, showering.) Might I want to keep an in-between journal? How do I listen to all that is within me, the light and the shadow, and extend unconditional love and care? How might I begin to transform through lovingly listening to all that is within? Might keeping a soul journal (with a group or on my own) help facilitate this inner listening, by exploring questions like the ones included in this chapter? When I look at my body through "gumball-eyes," how would I describe the love, light, stories, music, and entire worlds I house within? How might I like to pay attention to the role of healing in my life? Does healing feel like kindness and love? Is it difficult? Easy? What might a conversation sound like if I pulled up a chair and conversed with a presence of healing? To what degree have I hidden and revealed my vibrancy and light? Does my extent of sharing have something to do with my upbringing? Would I like to update my choices, given what I know now? What does it mean to shine my light and why might it matter? What have been some (divine) detours in my life, and what have I learned because of them? How have the detours formed the person I am becoming and want to be with? When I get silent and listen, what good company is near? Animals, neighbors, inner child, inner parts, loving words? Maybe even angels?

Notes & doodling

Rachel Awes offers

- book events and readings
  - speaking and listening
    - psychotherapy

She can be reached at

rachelawes@gmail.com

and rachelawes.com

Thank you

my wise, inspiring, brave + beautiful clients ✿ SARK ✿ the purple guy ✿ mercy ✿ apple trees ✿ angels ✿ Ben Awes ✿ Childkris laughter ✿ Abe Awes ✿ Sam Awes ✿ Karen Carlson ✿ Tracy Verdugo ✿ Wise Ink Creative Publishing ✿ Amy Quale ✿ my inmost magic ✿ my spring wardrobe ✿ the fiery flamingo ✿ Divine Detours ✿ light ✿ Toni, Larry Steph, Patrice ✿ Gudrun Sjoden designs ✿ Kelly Rae Roberts ✿ Sue's apple pie ✿ my inner child ✿ dirt, water, + sunlight ✿ tomatoes ✿ the winds ✿ stars I can share me with ✿ elephants ✿ whales in water + air, just as ✿ bluebells ✿ splendid expression ✿ anemones ✿ loving your heart + loving my heart, all life in between ✿ holi-ness ✿ my inner gypsy ✿ my maker ✿ lilies + lilacs! ✿ shining stars ✿ my messy ✿ Annie Banani ✿ sloths ✿ as we are

235

Other books by Rachel Awes

All I Did Was Listen tells a story of the progression of wholeness and healing for everyone, through colorful drawings, prose-like reflections, and more inspiring quotes from Rachel's therapy clients.

Diving In is a visual and poetic invitation, using water as metaphor, to dive into the one life that is so beautifully yours.

These books can be found at rachelawes.com/shop.

The Great Green Okayness is a field guide to discovering the beautiful wildlife and uncommon magnificence within.

236